izzy and jack

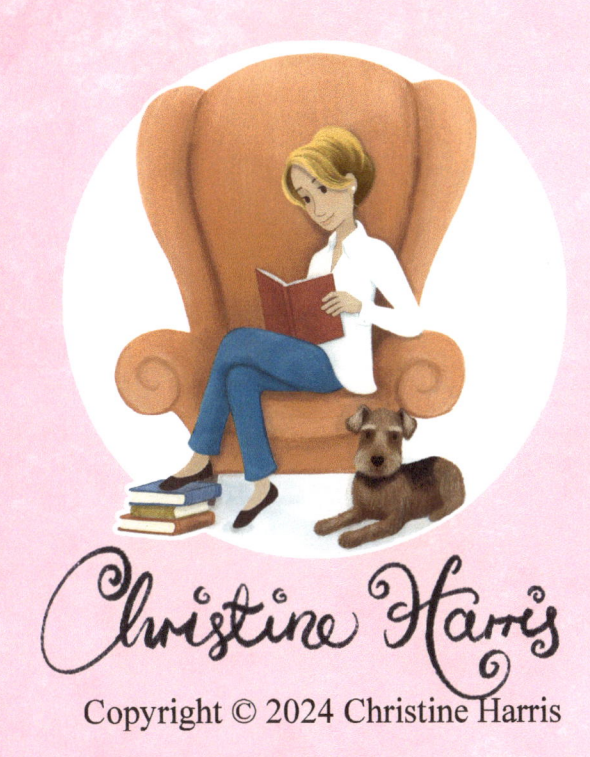

Published by Izzy and Jack
www.izzyandjack.co.uk

Christine Harris

Copyright © 2024 Christine Harris

All rights reserved.

This book or any portion thereof may not be reproduced or used in any manner whatsoever without the written permission of the publisher except for the use of brief quotations in a book review.

"Let Imagination Lead the Way to Adventure"

To all the boys and girls I've met,
taught, and shared stories with.

May your hearts always be full of wonder
and may you always find magic
in the pages of every book you read.

You've each left a mark on my heart,
and this story is for you.

In the starlit forest filled with magic and delight,

Bunny Valentine hops under the moon's gentle light.

She always comes home
with great tales to tell.

But this time
she's brought back
a suitcase as well.

Beside crystal-clear streams
and trees standing tall,

sits her warm,

cosy burrow,

not too big,
not too small.

Whispers echo
as friends grow excited.

Bunny thinks to herself,
"they'll be so delighted!"

They all try to guess.
"Bunny, what's in your case?
A map of some treasure where X marks the place?"

"Perhaps a spell to change the day!"

Chirps Bluebird in her merry way.

Night turns to day. What a magical sight,
Bunny's house glows in the shimmering light.

The creatures all plead, with joy in their eyes,

"Please open it!"

"Show us!"

"We want a surprise!"

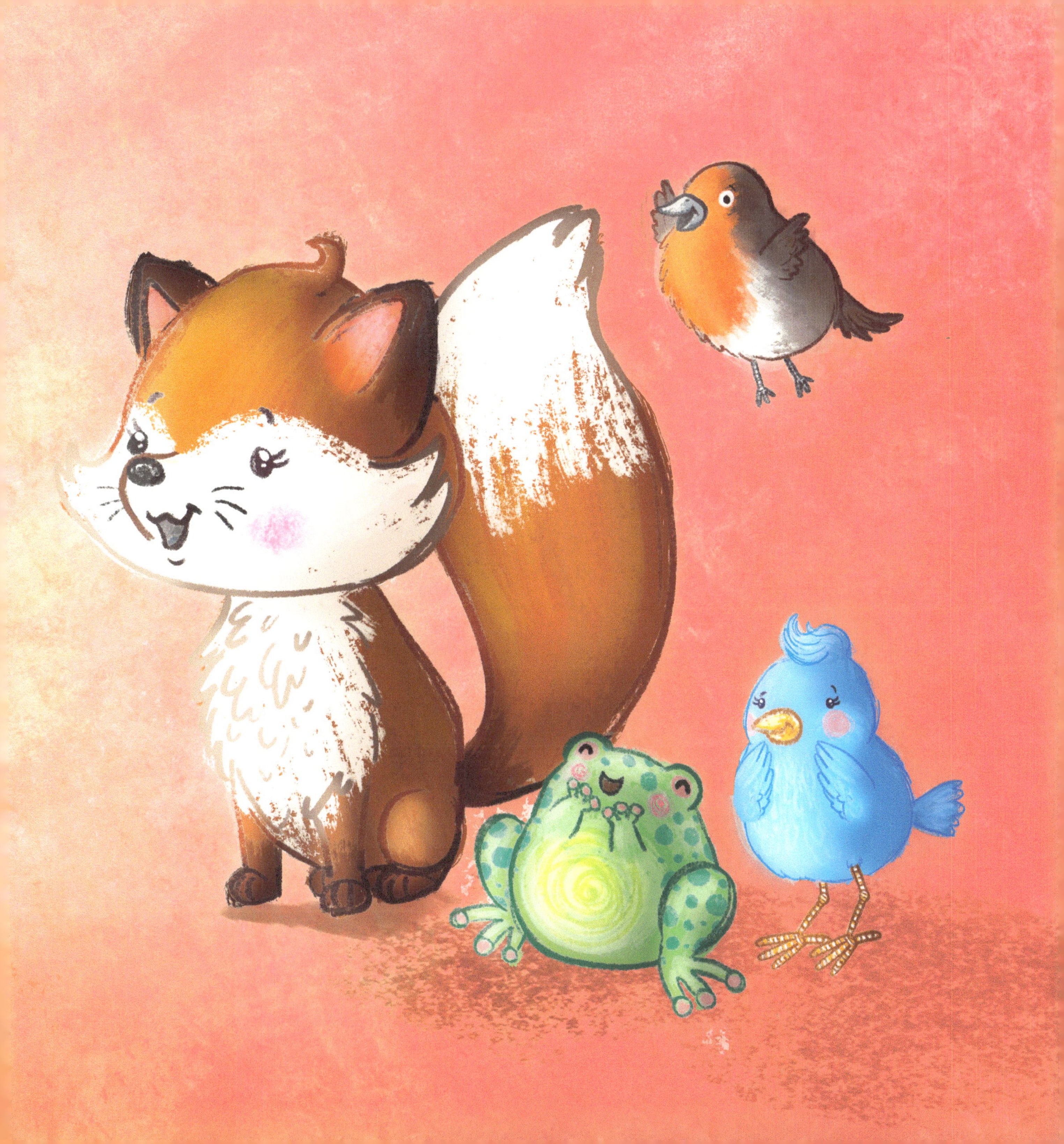

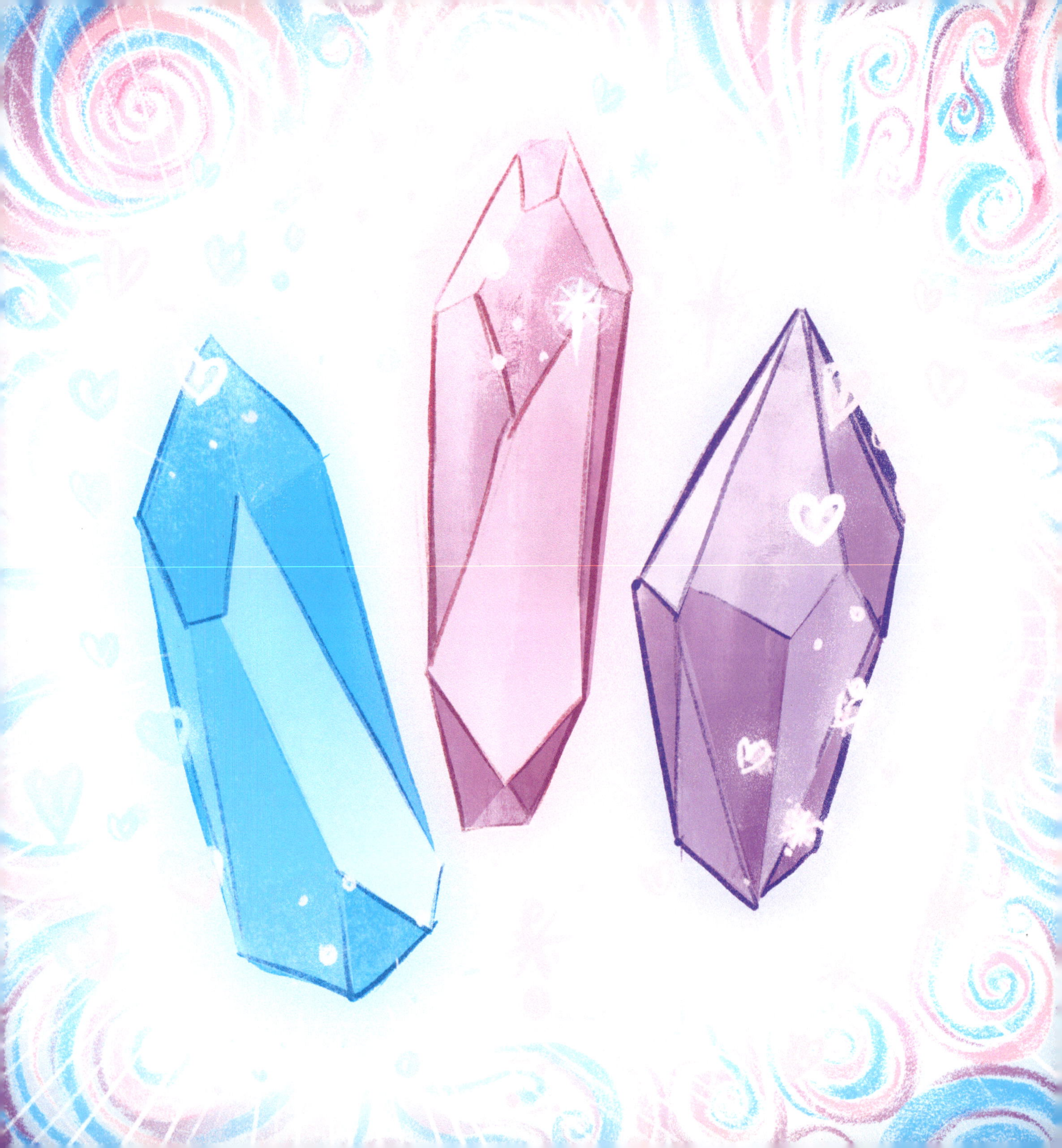

Bunny opens the case
to reveal what's inside.

It's three magic crystals,
neatly placed, side by side.

Sparkling, twinkling,
colours on display.
Casting their glow
in the bright light of day.

"I searched far and wide
to bring them to you.
These special crystals
can make dreams come true!"

"Friends, pick a crystal,
wish with all your might.
Close your eyes
and let the magic take flight."

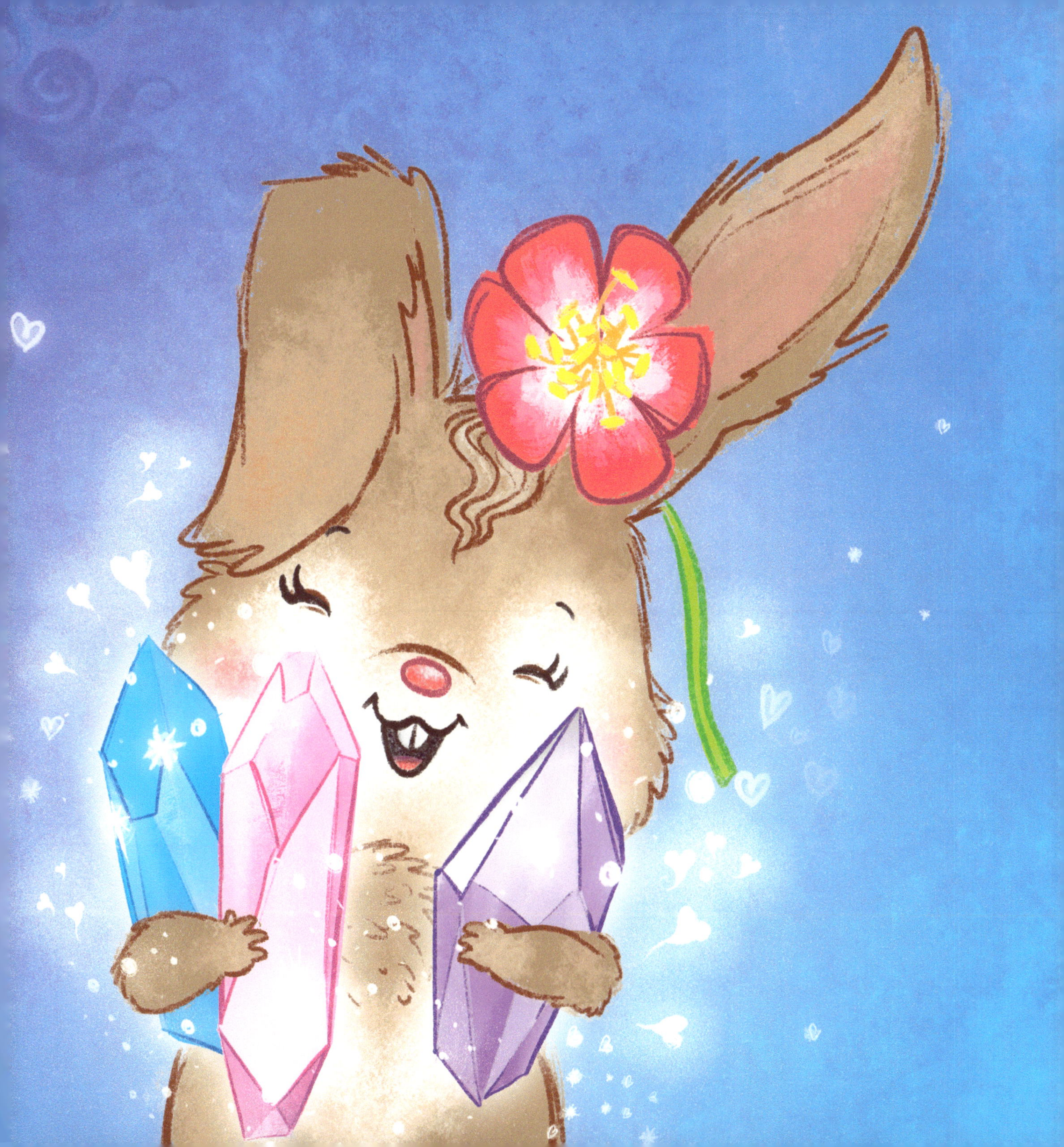

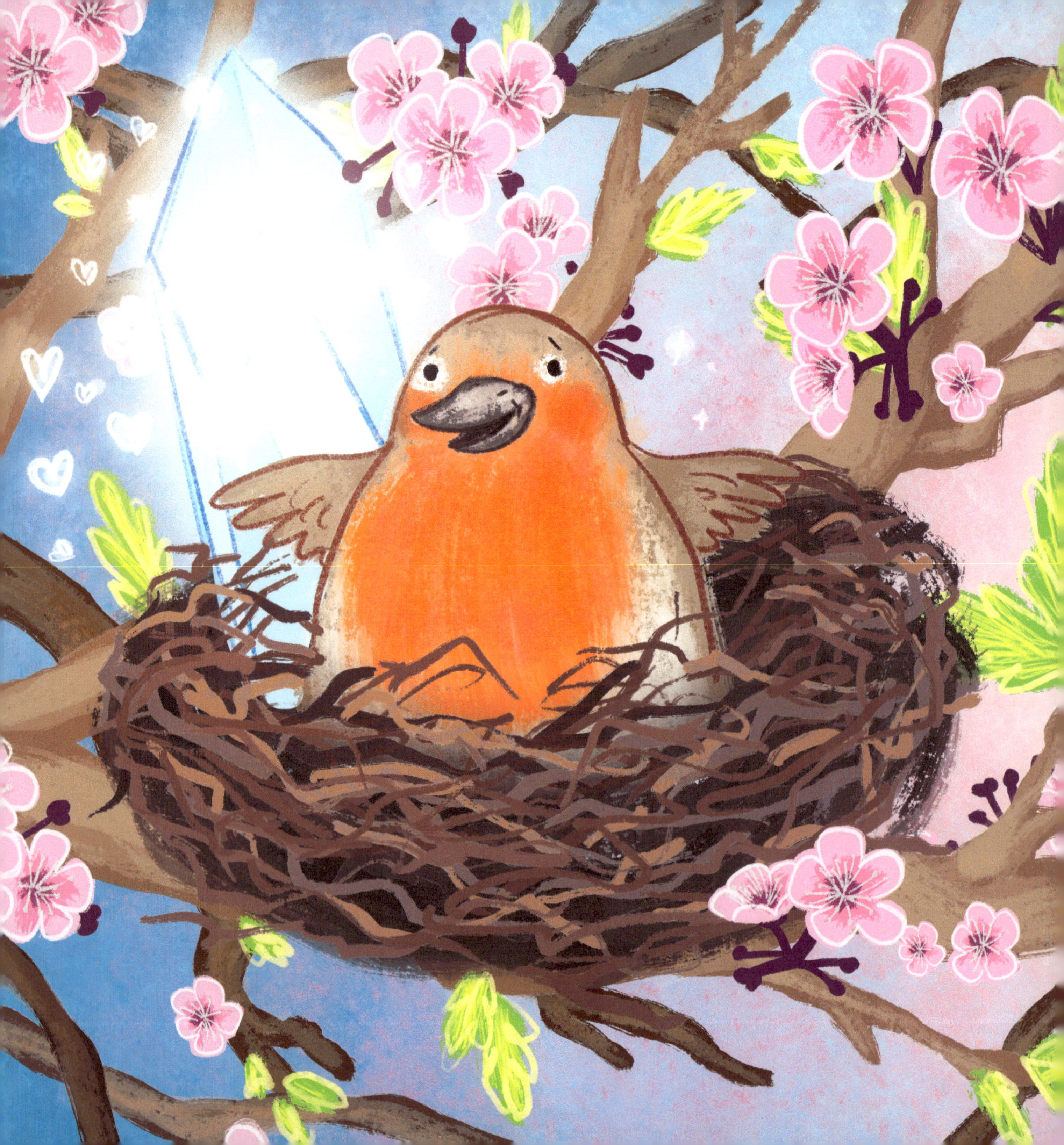

Daring, dear Robin, with his red feathered breast, dreams of the river from up in his nest.

"I've wanted forever to take a deep dive!"
He swoops down to the water.

His dreams come alive!

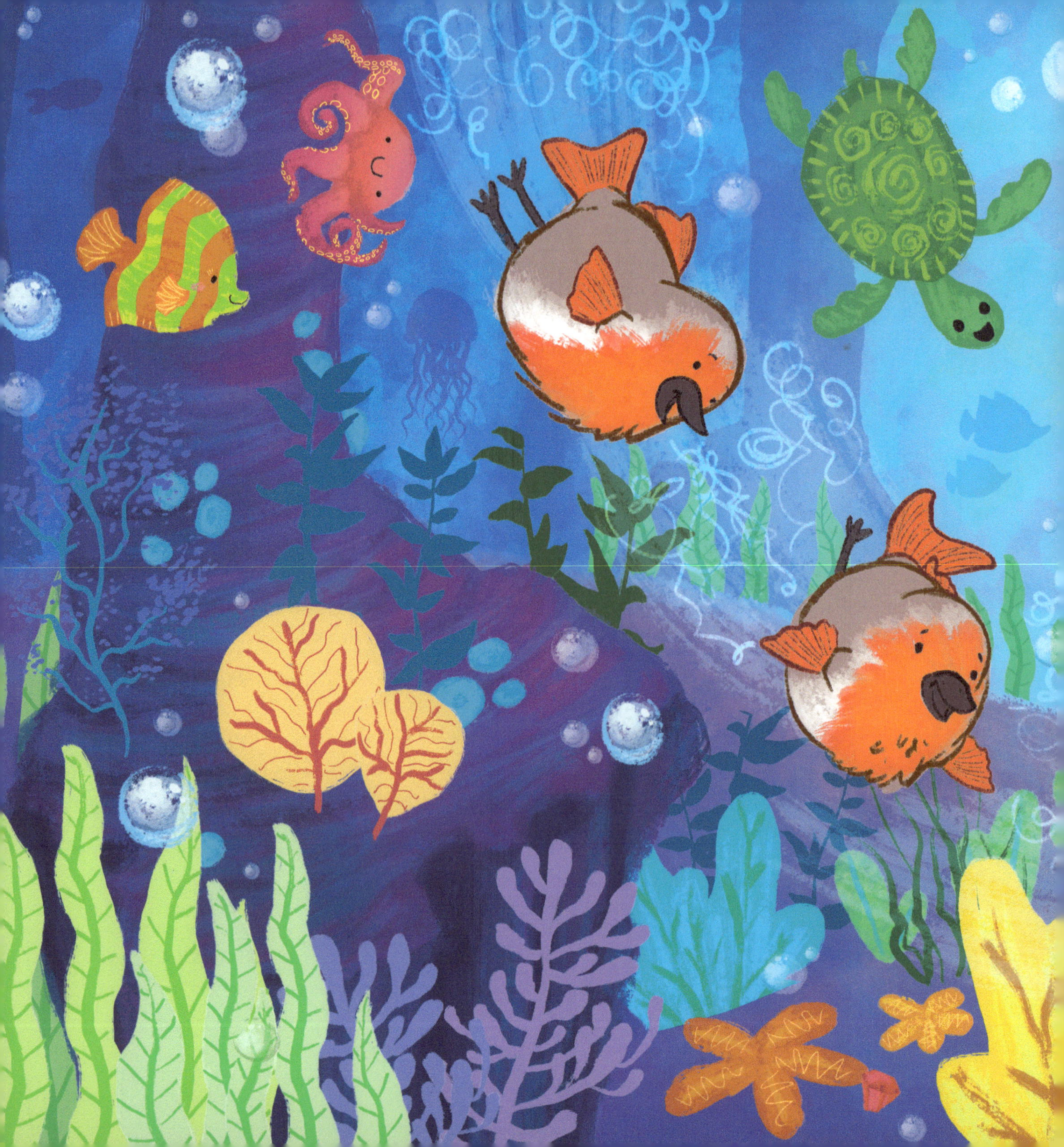

His wings become fins, oh what a sight!
in a world of wonder, his eyes wide and bright.
Stingrays and turtles, an underwater show,
caves and corals, colours that glow.

Dancing jellyfish light the way,
mermaids twirl and seahorses play.
Hidden treasures and jewels in the sand,
guarded by crabs and sea snails so grand.

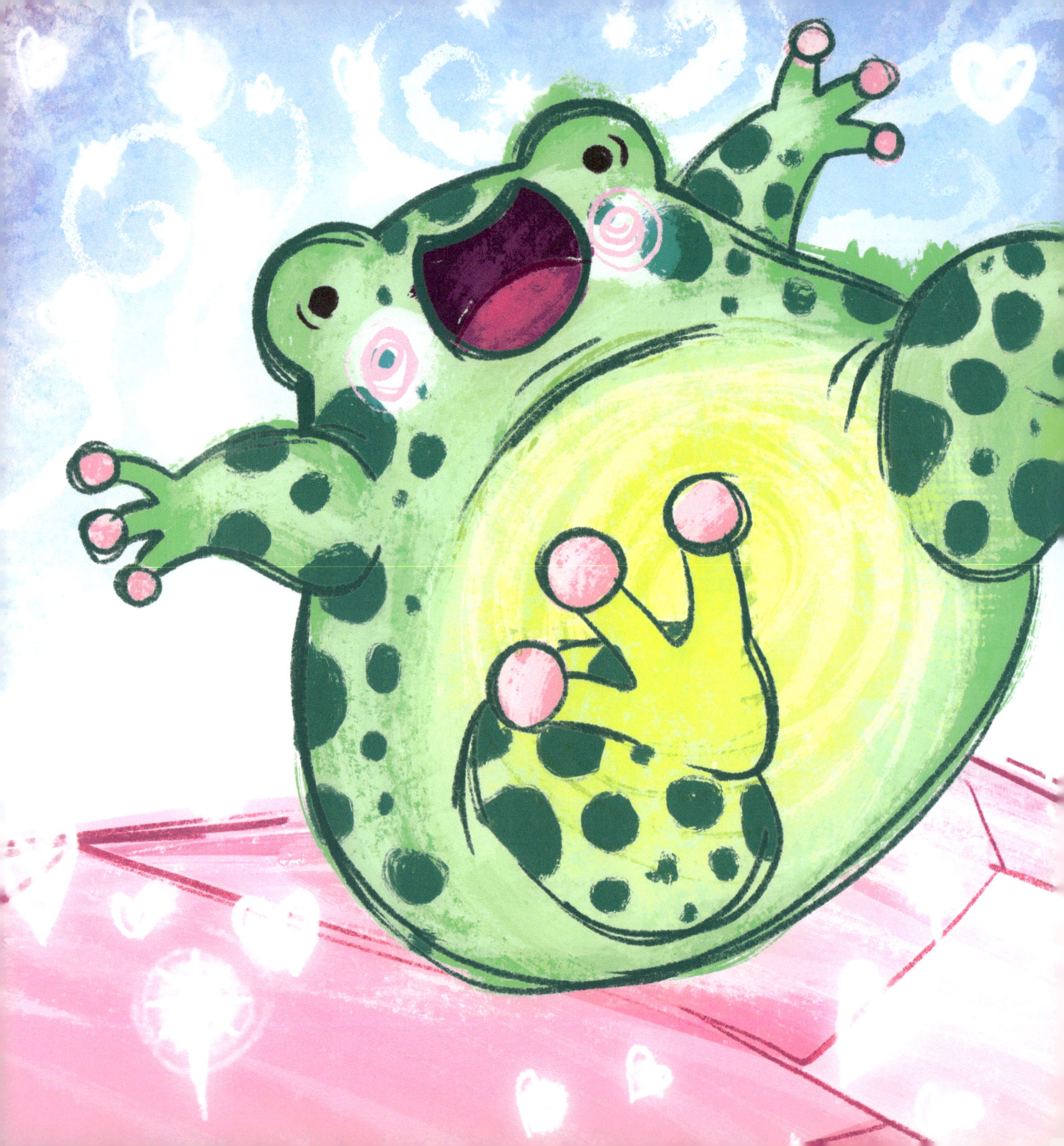

Frog wants to sing,
with a voice that's so sweet,
to no longer croak
would be such a treat!

"I wish on this crystal with all of my might"
and soon it begins to glow warmly and bright.

With a shimmer, Frog's carried not too far away,
to a meadow where dragonflies and wildflowers sway.

The meadow's alive with the buzzing of bees,
Frog takes a breath, and he lets out a sneeze.

He clears his throat with a quiver of fear,
His audience await, so eager to hear.

He sings with such passion,
his heart feels so light,
The notes dance on the breeze.
He sings into the night!

With the crystal's glow, Fox now wants a try,
"It's cloud-hopping for me! Please let me fly!"
She's given a map to help with her quest,
setting off for the mountains, she heads furthest west.

Climbing a cliff,
a breathtaking view,
heart racing,

excited,

her eyes shining, too.

With courage,
　　　　she leaps off,
gliding so high,

　　Soaring above
　　　　　valleys
　　with clouds
　　　　　passing by.

A glimmer,
a shimmer,
the magic aglow,

down rainbow slides,
how fast can she go?

Past a hot air balloon in the evening light,
with eagles soaring,
a magnificent sight!

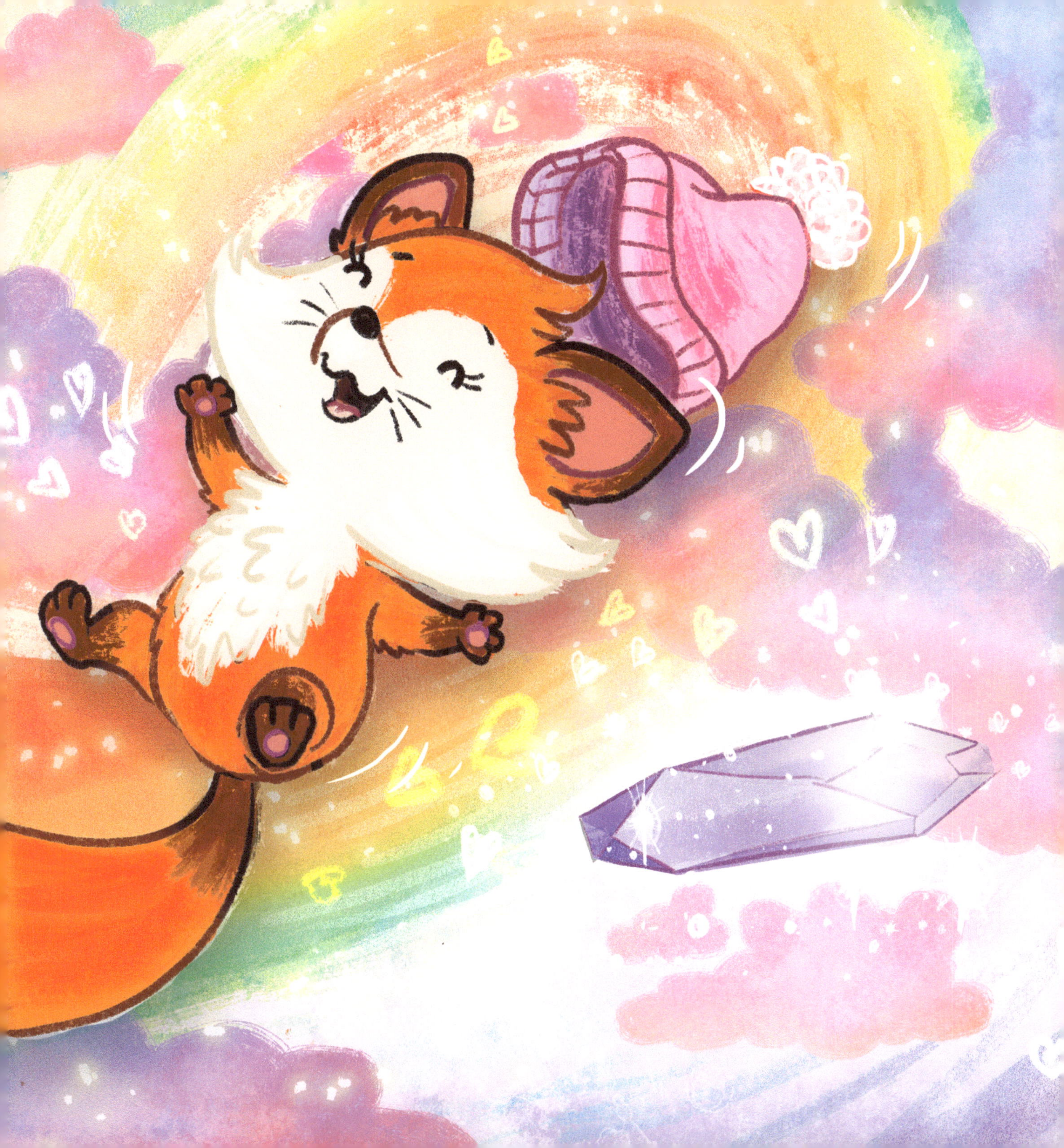

Then back at the burrow, in the moon's golden gleam,
the friends come together to share tales of their dreams.

Bunny's suitcase lays empty,
the crystals are gone.
She places little love hearts
in the space where they'd shone.

Under the moon,
they all laugh and play,
smiles,
magic,
and friendship,
lighting the way.

"Always keep dreaming,"
Bunny joyfully sings,

there's no need for crystals
        or sparkling things."

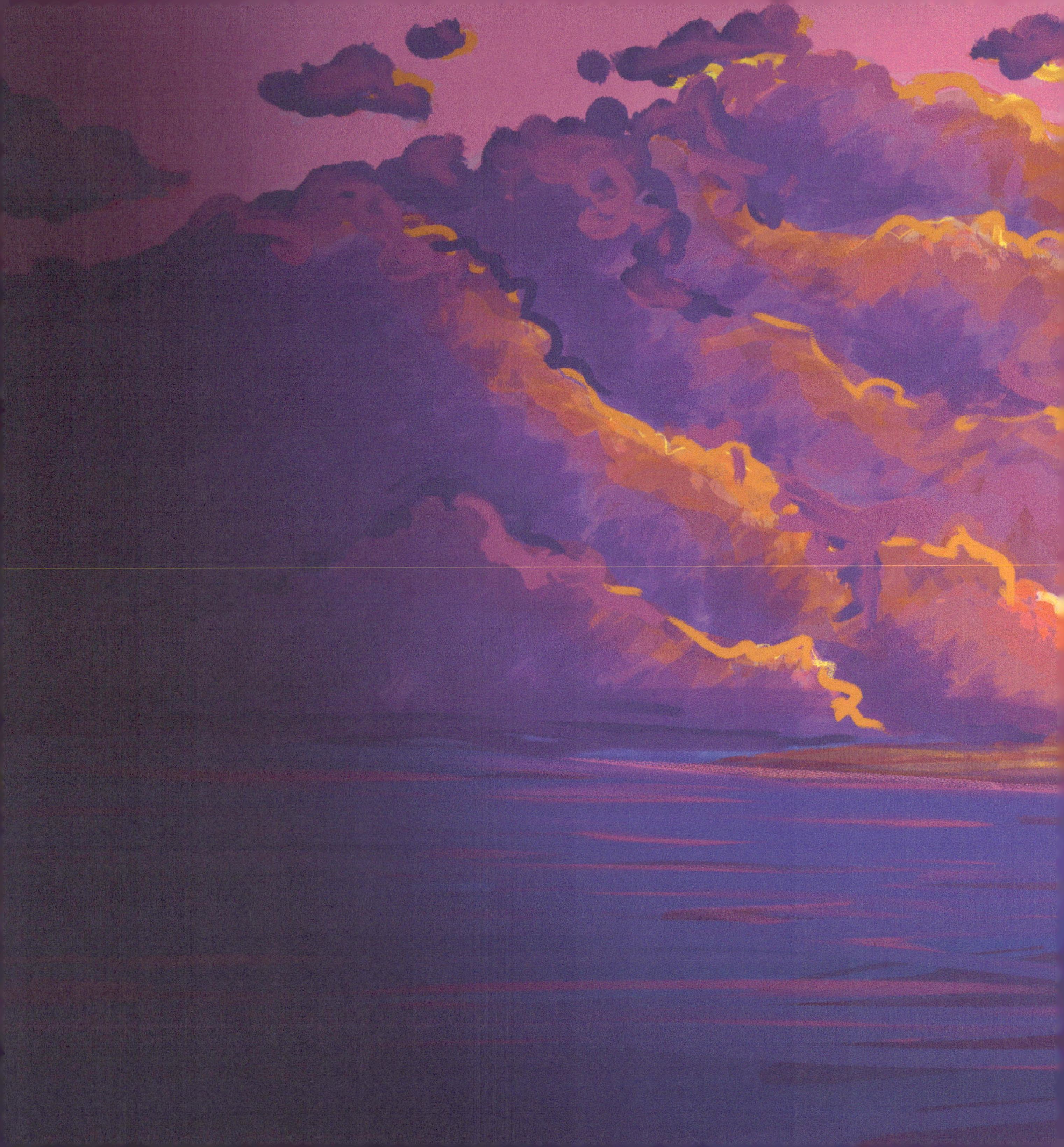

"Not all dreams
need magic for them
to come true.

Just follow your heart
and believe in you!"

Another beautiful story by Christine Harris to share with someone special.

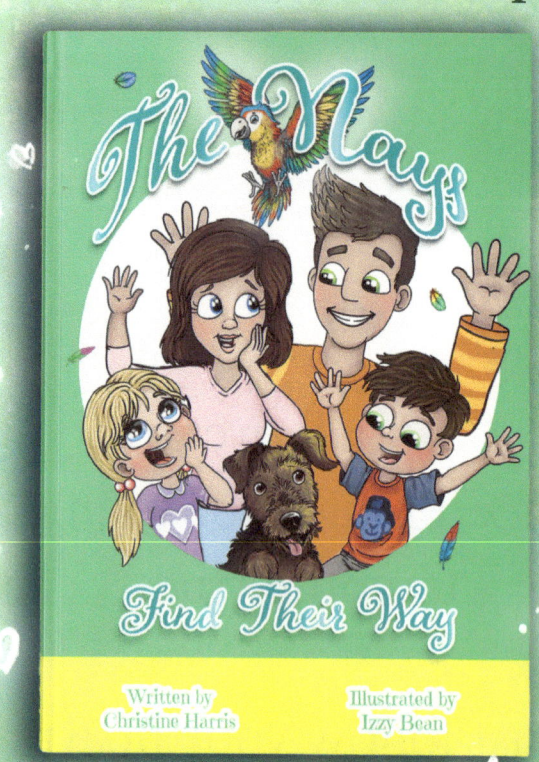

www.christineharrisbooks.com

Milton Keynes UK
Ingram Content Group UK Ltd.
UKHW052233051224
452053UK00009B/112